Saxon Math™
Intermediate 3–5

Calculator Activities

Stephen Hake

A Harcourt Achieve Imprint

www.SaxonPublishers.com
1-800-284-7019

Copyright © by Houghton Mifflin Harcourt Publishing Company

All rights reserved. No part of this work may be reproduced or transmitted in any form or by any means, electronic or mechanical, including photocopying or recording, or by any information storage or retrieval system, without the prior written permission of the copyright owner unless such copying is expressly permitted by federal copyright law.

Permission is hereby granted to individuals using the corresponding student's textbook or kit as the major vehicle for regular classroom instruction to photocopy entire pages from this publication in classroom quantities for instructional use and not for resale. Requests for information on other matters regarding duplication of this work should be addressed to Houghton Mifflin Harcourt Publishing Company, Attn: Contracts, Copyrights, and Licensing, 9400 South Park Center Loop, Orlando, Florida 32819.

Printed in the U.S.A.

ISBN 978-1-600-32354-6

4 5 6 7 8 9 10 1413 20 19 18 17 16 15 14 13 12

4500347581 ^ B C D E F G

> If you have received these materials as examination copies free of charge, Houghton Mifflin Harcourt Publishing Company retains title to the materials and they may not be resold. Resale of examination copies is strictly prohibited.

> Possession of this publication in print format does not entitle users to convert this publication, or any portion of it, into electronic format.

Table of Contents

Calculator Activities

Introduction iv

Content Chart v

Basic Calculator Use 1

Activity 1 • Addition 2
Teacher's Guide • Guided Practice • Practice Worksheets

Activity 2 • Subtraction 5
Teacher's Guide • Guided Practice • Practice Worksheets

Activity 3 • Money 8
Teacher's Guide • Guided Practice • Practice Worksheets

Activity 4 • Multiplication 13
Teacher's Guide • Guided Practice • Practice Worksheets

Activity 5 • Division 18
Teacher's Guide • Guided Practice • Practice Worksheets

Activity 6 • Fractions and Decimals. 21
Teacher's Guide • Guided Practice • Practice Worksheets

Activity 7 • Multiplying and Dividing Fractions . . 25
Teacher's Guide • Guided Practice • Practice Worksheets

Activity 8 • Order of Operations and Memory . . . 29
Teacher's Guide • Guided Practice • Practice Worksheets

Activity 9 • Area and Volume 33
Teacher's Guide • Guided Practice • Practice Worksheets

Activity 10 • Supplementary Exercises 37
Teacher's Guide • Practice Worksheets

Answers to Exercises. 41

Saxon Math   © Harcourt Achieve Inc. and Stephen Hake. All rights reserved.   iii

Introduction

About the Calculator Activities

At Saxon Publishers, we believe that people learn by doing. Students learn mathematics not by watching or listening to others, but by doing the problems themselves. Integration of technology into any curriculum is important for students to be competitive in a constantly changing academic landscape. Technology, like calculators, can be helpful tools that allow students to step away from the arithmetic and explore a deeper level of mathematics.

Calculator Technologies and the Language of Mathematics

Throughout grades 3–5, students must learn to incorporate language and reasoning with technology to develop conceptual understandings and solve problems. By itself, the basic 4-function calculator is a simple technology that quickly processes addition, subtraction, multiplication and division facts. Only when the language of mathematics is integrated into its function and there is reasoning and logic to its use does the simple calculator rise to the level of a true educational tool. Students learn the logic and process of mathematics through the creation of calculator equations they enter on their keypads to solve problems. By thinking out loud as they enter keystrokes, students make use of the language of mathematics.

Structure and Guidelines

This manual is divided into sections that demonstrate the calculator's usefulness in solving various types of mathematical problems. It is recommended that teachers preview the entire lesson, practicing the example problems on their own.

Each section begins with a **teacher's guide**. The teacher's guide provides vocabulary essential to the lesson as well as the basics for performing the operations on the calculator, and tips for avoiding errors and making the lesson run smoothly.

The calculator activities in the **guided practice** sections are designed for whole-class instruction that leads into individual and group practice. This section provides example problems and their step-by-step instructions.

Finally, each section has a reproducible **practice worksheet** with problems relevant to the lesson. Students should complete these problems independently.

iv   © Harcourt Achieve Inc. and Stephen Hake. All rights reserved.   *Saxon Math*

Lesson Correspondence

The following tables offer textbook lessons that correspond to the activities in the calculator manual. The supplementary activities cover a variety of topics found throughout the text.

Grade 3

Calculator Activity	Lessons
1 – Addition	Lesson 16
2 – Subtraction	Lesson 19
4 – Multiplication	Lesson 60
5 – Division	Lesson 101
9 – Area and Volume	Lesson 73

Grade 4

Calculator Activity	Lessons
1 – Addition	Lesson 2
3 – Money	Lessons 22, 91
4 – Multiplication	Lesson 87
5 – Division	Lesson 46
6 – Fractions and Decimals	Lessons 84, 112
9 – Area and Volume	Lesson Inv. 3
Supplementary Exercises	Lesson 57, Inv. 6

Saxon Math © Harcourt Achieve Inc. and Stephen Hake. All rights reserved.

Lesson Correspondence

Grade 5

Calculator Activity	Lessons
1 – Addition	Lesson 11
2 – Subtraction	Lesson 16
3 – Money	Lessons 13, 49
4 – Multiplication	Lesson 51
5 – Division	Lesson 22
6 – Fractions and Decimals	Lesson 81, Inv. 3
7 – Multiplying and Dividing Fractions	Lessons 76, 96
8 – Order of Operations and Memory	Lesson 24
9 – Area and Volume	Lesson 72
Supplementary Exercises	Lesson 89, Inv. 5

Introduction

Basic Calculator Use:

Number Pad Keys

Use these keys to enter digits.

You will see instructions such as:

Enter the number: 3 7 4

Press the keys

[3] [7] [4]

The calculator will display:

374

Operation Keys

Use these keys to perform operations of adding, subtracting, multiplying, and dividing. The equals key shows the result of the last operation performed.

Enter the equation 4 + 3 =

Press the keys

[4] [+] [3] [Enter/=]

The calculator will display:

7

Memory Keys

Use these keys to store values in memory when working multiple step problems.

There is an entire section of lessons devoted to the use of memory keys. Refer to that section for guidelines and practice.

Addition 1

• Add 2 or More Numbers

Teacher's Guide

Vocabulary:

Addend, sum, total

The answer to an addition problem is called the **sum** or **total**. The numbers being added are called the **addends**.

Example: 2 + 3 = 5: The **sum** of the **addends** 2 and 3 is 5.

Operation:

Basic addition with a calculator is straightforward. Most students will already know how to perform this operation.

Tips:

Remind students that the **last** number they enter before pressing the = key remains in memory. You can keep adding that same number to the total by pressing the = key.

Repeated addition is excellent for exercises in skip-counting or for recall of multiplication tables.

Enter 5 + 2 =	Display
(5) (+) (2) (Enter =)	7
Enter =	
(Enter =)	9
Enter =	
(Enter =)	11
Enter =	
(Enter =)	13

The calculator will continue to add **2** each time the = key is pressed.

2 © Harcourt Achieve Inc. and Stephen Hake. All rights reserved. *Saxon Math*

Addition 1

Guided Practice

Add two numbers: To add 2 numbers, enter the digits of the first number, then press the **ADD** operation key, enter the digits of the second number and then press the = key. The answer will be displayed.

Example: Add 32 + 256

Enter the following:

[3] [2] [+] [2] [5] [6] [Enter/=] | 288 |

Adding more than two numbers: To add more than 2 numbers, enter the digits of the first number, press the + key, enter the digits of the second number, and again press the + key. Continue entering numbers and pressing the + key until you enter the last number. Press the = key after the last number.

Example: Add 5 + 7 + 9 + 21

Enter the following:

[5] [+] [7] [+] [9] [+] [2] [1] [Enter/=] | 42 |

Repeating Addition, Skip Counting. You can continue to add the same number to your total without entering it again. Press the = key for as many times as you wish to add that number.

Example: Add 6 *three times* to 21.

Enter 21

[2] [1] [Enter/=] | 21 |

Add 6

[+] [6] [Enter/=] | 27 |

Repeat add 6

[Enter/=] | 33 |

Repeat add 6

[Enter/=] | 39 |

Saxon Math

Name _____

Addition 1
Practice Worksheet

Add the following 2 digit numbers with your calculator:

Example: Add 21 + 39

Enter: 21 + 39 =

[2][1][+][3][9][Enter =]

| 60 |

The answer is **60**

1. 37 + 82 = _____
2. 19 + 77 = _____
3. 66 + 88 = _____
4. 44 + 33 = _____
5. 91 + 12 = _____
6. 21 + 42 = _____

Add this series of one digit numbers and write your answer:

7. 9 + 7 + 2 + 4 + 1 + 5 = _____

Skip count the following:

Example: Count up by 3s from 12 to 21.

Enter: 12 + 3 =

[1][2][+][3][Enter =]

| 15 |

=

| 18 |

=

| 21 |

15 18 21

8. Count up by 5s starting at 22.   22, _____, _____, _____

9. Count up by 7s starting at 14.   14, _____, _____, _____

10. Chloe is collecting canned goods for a food drive at school. She started with 3 cans at the beginning of the day. The following table lists Chloe's friends and how many cans of food they each brought in to school. How many cans of food did Chloe and her friends bring in?

Name	# of cans
Veronica	8
Josh	6
Monique	4
Terrell	7

_____

4   © Harcourt Achieve Inc. and Stephen Hake. All rights reserved.   Saxon Math

Subtraction 2

• Subtract 2 or More Numbers

Teacher's Guide

Vocabulary:

Difference

When we **subtract** two numbers we find the **difference**.

Operation:

Basic subtraction with a calculator is straightforward. Most students will already know how to perform this operation.

Tips:

Remind students that the **last** number they enter before striking the = key remains in memory and can be used to keep subtracting that same number from the total.

Repeated subtraction is excellent for exercises in skip-counting.

	Display
Enter 15 − 3 =	
1 5 − 3 Enter=	12
Enter =	
Enter=	9
Enter =	
Enter=	6
Enter =	
Enter=	3

The calculator will continue to subtract by **2** each time the = key is pressed.

Guided Practice

Subtract two numbers: To subtract 2 numbers, enter the digits of the first number, then press the (−) operation key, enter the digits of the second number, and then press the = key.

Saxon Math © Harcourt Achieve Inc. and Stephen Hake. All rights reserved. 5

Subtraction 2

Example: Subtract 22 − 13

Enter the following:

(2) (2) (−) (1) (3) (Enter =)

| 9 |

Subtracting two or more numbers from an amount: You can subtract two or more numbers from a beginning amount by continuing to press the (−) and entering numbers to subtract. When you have entered your last number to subtract, enter the = key.

Example: Subtract 24 − 7 − 9

Enter the following:

(2) (4) (−) (7) (−) (9) (Enter =)

| 8 |

Repeating Subtraction, Skip Counting. You can continue to subtract the same number from your total without entering it again. Press the = key for as many times as you wish to subtract that number.

Example: Subtract 6 *three times* from 21, view each subtraction:

Enter 21

(2) (1) (Enter =)

| 21 |

Subtract 6

(−) (6) (Enter =)

| 15 |

Repeat subtract 6

(Enter =)

| 9 |

Repeat subtract 6

(Enter =)

| 3 |

6 © Harcourt Achieve Inc. and Stephen Hake. All rights reserved. *Saxon Math*

Name _____

Subtraction 2
Practice Worksheet

Subtract the following 2 digit numbers with your calculator:

Example: Subtract 65 − 39

Enter: 65 − 39

(6)(5)(−)(3)(9)(Enter/=)   26

The answer is **26**

1. 82 − 37 = _____   2. 77 − 19 = _____   3. 88 − 66 = _____

4. 44 − 33 = _____   5. 91 − 12 = _____   6. 42 − 21 = _____

7. 36 − 36 = _____   8. 84 − 15 = _____   9. 43 − 34 = _____

Subtract this series of numbers and write your answer:

10. 98 − 37 − 22 − 14 − 8 − 5 = _____

Skip count the following:

Example: Count down by 3s from 24 to 15.

Enter: 24 − 3 =

(2)(4)(−)(3)(Enter/=)   21

=   18

=   15

24 **21 18 15**

11. Count down by 5s starting at 22.   22, _____, _____, _____

12. Count down by 7s starting at 35.   35, _____, _____, _____

13. Ari decided to give away some of his baseball card collection. He had 50 cards and gave 13 to Tanya, 7 to Luke, and 20 to Jamaal. How many cards does Ari have left?

_____

Saxon Math   © Harcourt Achieve Inc. and Stephen Hake. All rights reserved.   7

• Adding and Subtracting Money

Teacher's Guide

Vocabulary:
Dollars, cents, place value, ones/tens/hundreds place, decimal point, tenths/hundredths place

Operation:
Adding or subtracting money is similar to adding or subtracting regular numbers. Students need to understand place value in order to enter dollars and cents correctly.

Dollars correspond with the ones, tens, hundreds and higher place values.

Entry of a decimal point is critical for all calculations with cents.

Tips:
For even dollar amounts, you do not need to enter a decimal point and two zeros.

For example, you can enter the amount of $10 with [1] [0] only.

$10 can also be entered as: [1] [0] [.] [0] [0]

You may wish to have your students add the extra digits after the decimal point to remember place order and since money always appears in places like cash registers with dollars AND cents.

You may want to have students work with amounts that have similar digits but different place values such as $20.50, $25.00, $20.05 to emphasize the importance of the decimal point and place value.

Guided Practice

When we use the basic calculator to add or subtract money, the numbers we use for the calculator must be in dollars and cents form. Dollars are entered in the calculator using the ones, tens and hundreds place values. To enter cents, you must first enter the decimal point (.) and then enter the cents.

Example 1: Add $378.25 + $196.38

Solution: Our money is already in dollar-and-cents form.

$378.25 + $196.38 =

③ ⑦ ⑧ · ② ⑤ ➕ ① ⑨ ⑥ · ③ ⑧ [Enter =] | 574.63 |

$378.25 plus $196.38 is $574.63

Example 2: Eduardo and Ramon combined their penny collections. Eduardo had 63 pennies. Ramon had 72 pennies.

  a. How many pennies did they have together?

  b. How much money did they have together?

Solution 2a: To find the number of pennies we add 63 and 72.

63 + 72 =

⑥ ③ ➕ ⑦ ② [Enter =] | 135 |

Eduardo and Ramon together had 135 pennies.

Solution 2b: To find how much money Eduardo and Ramon had we must first convert the cents to dollars-and-cents.

Enter: $0.63 + $0.72 =

⓪ · ⑥ ③ ➕ ⓪ · ⑦ ② [Enter =] | 1.35 |

We read this answer as one dollar and 35 cents.
Ramon and Eduardo together have $1.35.

Example 3: What is the value of the money shown below?

To add a collection of money, we group it by value, and enter the value of each item in dollar-and-cents format, using a decimal point. We enter:

$1.00 + $1.00 + $0.25 + $0.25 + $0.10 + $0.10 + $0.10 + $0.10 + $0.10 + $0.01 + $0.01 =

In the calculator we enter:

1 . 0 0 + 1 . 0 0 + (dollars)   2.00

0 . 2 5 + 0 . 2 5 + (quarters)   2.50

0 . 1 0 + 0 . 1 0 +

0 . 1 0 + 0 . 1 0 +

0 . 1 0 + (dimes)   3.00

0 . 0 1 + 0 . 0 1 Enter (pennies)   3.02

The display tells us the money equals three dollars and two cents. **The answer is $3.02.**

Example 4: Subtract: $378.25 − $196.38

Solution: Our money is already in dollar-and-cents form.

$378.25 − $196.38 =

3 7 8 . 2 5 − 1 9 6 . 3 8 Enter   181.87

$378.25 minus $196.38 is $181.87

Example 5: Eduardo and Ramon combined their penny collections. Together they had 135 pennies. Ramon took his 72 pennies home.

   a. How many pennies did Eduardo have left?

   b. How much money does Eduardo have?

Money **3**

Solution 5a: To find the number of pennies left we subtract 72 from 135

$$135 - 72 =$$

(1)(3)(5)(−)(7)(2)(Enter =) | 63 |

Eduardo has 63 pennies.

Solution 5b: To find how much money Eduardo has we must convert the cents to dollars-and-cents.

Enter $1.35 − $0.72 =

(1)(·)(3)(5)(−)(0)(·)(7)(2)(Enter =) | 63 |

Example 6: Charles has $135.00 for school clothes. He bought a shirt for $29.95 and pants for $14.95. How much money does he have left?

Solution: We enter

$$\$135.00 - \$29.95 - \$14.95 =$$

(1)(3)(5)(·)(0)(0)(−) | 135.00 |

(2)(9)(·)(9)(5)(−) | 105.05 |

(1)(4)(·)(9)(5)(Enter =) | 90.1 |

The display tells us Charles has 90.1 dollars left. To understand this answer, we must remember that you can add a zero at the right of tenths place digit of the calculator without changing its value. **Charles has $90.10.**

Saxon Math   © Harcourt Achieve Inc. and Stephen Hake. All rights reserved.   **11**

Name _____

Money 3
Practice Worksheet

1. How much is $572.23 plus $488.99? _____

2. How much is $245.32 minus $135.50? _____

3. How much is 32 pennies plus one dollar plus two quarters?

   _____

4. What is the value of the money shown below? _____

5. Peggy's parents spent $73 at the shoe store. Peggy's shoes cost $24, and her sister Sharon's shoes also cost $24. The rest of the money was spent on her brother Logan's shoes. How much was spent on Logan's shoes? Mark your answer.

   A $49   **B** $27   **C** $48   **D** $25

6. Bernie has exactly $8.00. He wants to write home to his parents while visiting his aunt. He needs supplies from the list shown below. All prices include tax.

Stamps (book of 5)	$2.00	Pen	$0.89
Envelopes (pack of 10)	$1.89	Pencil	$0.59
Writing Pad	$3.29	Eraser	$0.29
Tape	$1.99		

   Which of the following combinations does Bernie not have enough money to buy?

   A envelopes, stamps, pencil, and writing pad

   B eraser, tape, pencil, and writing pad

   C pen, stamps, envelopes, and writing pad

   D pencil, envelopes, eraser, and tape

12 © Harcourt Achieve Inc. and Stephen Hake. All rights reserved.   Saxon Math

Multiplication 4

• Multiplying Numbers

Teacher's Guide

Vocabulary:

Factor, product, inches, feet, yards

Numbers being multiplied are called **factors**. The answer to a multiplication problem is called the **product**.

> **Example:** $8 \times 10 = 80$: 8 and 10 are the **factors** and 80 is the **product**.

Operation:

Perform basic multiplication on a calculator by entering one factor, then the multiply key ($\times$), the other factor and then the equal sign ($=$). The answer on the display is the product.

Students can multiply to change from one unit of measurement to another. The guided practice offers examples using length, but similar steps can be applied to convert units of mass and volume as well.

Tips:

When performing repeated multiplication, the **first** factor will be the repeating factor. This is different from the other operations that repeat the **second** number.

For example, to multiply 5×2 and then continue to multiply by the result by 5, you enter the **5** first.

	Display
Enter $5 \times 2 =$ [5] [x] [2] [Enter =]	10
Enter $=$ [Enter =]	50
Enter $=$ [Enter =]	250

The calculator will continue to multiply by **5** each time the $=$ key is pressed.

Saxon Math © Harcourt Achieve Inc. and Stephen Hake. All rights reserved. 13

Multiplication 4

Guided Practice

Multiplying 2 or More Numbers

Multiplying 2 or more numbers: To multiply 2 or more numbers, enter the digits of the first number, then press the (×) operation key, enter the digits of the second number and then press the = key.

Example: Multiply 25 × 13

2 5 × 1 3 Enter=

| 325 |

Multiply 12 × 15 × 6

2 5 × 1 5 × 6 Enter=

| 1080 |

Repeated Multiplication

You can continue to multiply by the same number by pressing the = key for as many times as you wish to multiply. When you press the = key your answer will multiply by the **first** number that you typed in, not the second.

Multiply 36 × 4, then continue to multiply by 4 three more times.

Step 1: Enter:

4 × 3 6 Enter=

| 144 |

Step 2: Enter:

Enter=

| 576 |

Step 3: Enter:

Enter=

| 2304 |

Step 4: Enter:

Enter=

| 9216 |

Each result is multiplied by **4** not **36**.

14   © Harcourt Achieve Inc. and Stephen Hake. All rights reserved.   *Saxon Math*

Multiplication 4

Measurement Conversion Tables

Use your calculator to make conversion tables of yards to feet and feet to inches.

Remember: There are 12 inches in one foot.
There are 3 feet in one yard.

To convert yards to feet, multiply the number of yards × 3.

Example 1: Convert 5 yards to feet.

Solution: Multiply the number of yards (5) times 3.

Enter: 5 × 3 =

[5] [×] [3] [Enter/=] | 15 |

There are 15 feet in 5 yards.

Example 2: Convert 4 feet to inches.

Solution: Multiply the number of feet (4) × 12.

Enter: 4 × 12 =

[4] [×] [1] [2] [Enter/=] | 48 |

There are 48 inches in 4 feet.

Example 3: Convert 3 yards to inches.

Solution: Multiply the number of yards times 3 to get the number of feet. Multiply the number of feet times 12 to get inches.

Enter: 3 × 3 =

[3] [×] [3] [Enter/=] | 9 |

There are **9 feet** in 3 yards.

Enter: 9 × 12 =

[9] [×] [1] [2] [Enter/=] | 108 |

There are 108 inches in 3 yards.

Saxon Math   © Harcourt Achieve Inc. and Stephen Hake. All rights reserved.   **15**

Name _____

Multiplication 4
Practice Worksheet

Multiply the following numbers with your calculator:

Example: Multiply 8 × 9

Enter: 8 × 9 =

[8] [x] [9] [Enter =]

| | 72 |

1. 6 × 5 = _____   **2.** 3 × 4 = _____   **3.** 7 × 8 = _____

4. 25 × 25 = _____   **5.** 30 × 30 = _____   **6.** 11 × 43 = _____

Example: Multiply 9 × 3 × 3 × 3 × 3

Enter: 3 × 9 =

[3] [x] [9] [Enter =]

| | 27 |

=

[Enter =]

| | 81 |

=

[Enter =]

| | 243 |

=

[Enter =]

| | 729 |

7. Multiply 8 × 4 × 4 × 4 × 4

_____ _____ _____ _____

8. The basketball team made 54 baskets in their last game and scored 72 points. Each basket was worth either one point or two points. How many one-point and two-point baskets did the team make?

A 30 two-point baskets and 24 one-point baskets

B 18 two-point baskets and 36 one-point baskets

C 14 two-point baskets and 40 one-point baskets

D 27 two-point baskets and 27 one-point baskets

16   © Harcourt Achieve Inc. and Stephen Hake. All rights reserved.   *Saxon Math*

Name _____

Multiplication 4

Practice Worksheet (cont.)

9. Individual bags of chips for the school cafeteria come in boxes of 12. If the cafeteria orders 100 boxes of chips, how many bags will they have?

   A 1012 bags **B** 121 bags **C** 1200 bags **D** 112 bags

10. Fill in the tables below to make your own personal conversion chart.

Yards to Feet to Inches

Yards	Feet	Inches
1	3	36
2	6	
3		
4		
5		

Feet to Inches

Feet	Inches
1	12
2	24
3	
4	
5	

Gallons to Quarts to Pints

Gallons	Quarts	Pints
1	4	8
2	8	
3		
4		
5		

Pounds to Ounces

Pounds	Ounces
1	16
2	32
3	
4	
5	

11. Gabrielle measured rooms in her house and learned that her bedroom is 8 feet long and 12 feet wide. How long and how wide is Gabrielle's bedroom in inches?

_____

Saxon Math © Harcourt Achieve Inc. and Stephen Hake. All rights reserved.

Division 5

• Dividing Numbers

Teacher's Guide

Vocabulary:

Dividend, divisior, quotient

"**A group of** (dividend) **divided into** (divisor) **equal parts has** (quotient) members **in each part.**"

Example: "A group of 63, divided into 9 equal parts, has 7 members in each part."

Operation:

Perform basic division on a calculator by entering the dividend (number to be divided), the division key (÷), the divisor number and finally the equal key (=).

Tips:

You can continue to divide by the same number without entering it again. Press the = key for as many times as you wish to divide.

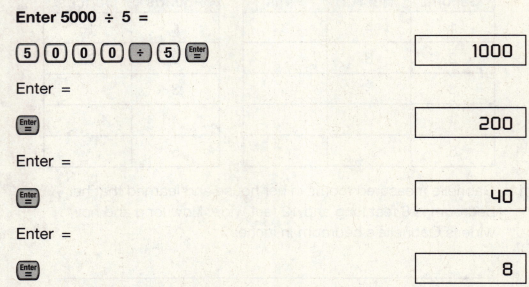

The calculator will continue to divide by **5** each time the = key is pressed.

Division 5

Guided Practice

Dividing

To divide 2 numbers, enter the digits of the first number as the dividend (the number to be divided), then press the (÷) key, enter the digits of the second number as the divisor (the number you will divide by) and then press the = key.

Example:

Divide: $25 \div 5$

[2] [5] [÷] [5] [Enter =]

	5

Repeated Division

The number that will be used repeatedly to divide must be entered **last**. Repeated division works just like repeated addition and subtraction.

Divide: $3125 \div 5$, four times and view results

Step 1:

[3] [1] [2] [5] [÷] [5] [Enter =]

	625

Step 2: Enter:

[Enter =]

	125

Step 3: Enter:

[Enter =]

	25

Step 4: Enter:

[Enter =]

	5

Saxon Math © Harcourt Achieve Inc. and Stephen Hake. All rights reserved. **19**

Name _____

Division 5
Practice Worksheet

Divide the following numbers with your calculator:

   Example: Divide 45 ÷ 9

   Enter: 45 ÷ 9

   [4] [5] [÷] [9] [Enter/=] | 5 |

   The answer is 5

Divide the following numbers with your calculator:

1. 12 ÷ 3 = _____
2. 24 ÷ 8 = _____
3. 50 ÷ 5 = _____
4. 99 ÷ 11 = _____
5. 144 ÷ 12 = _____
6. 875 ÷ 25 = _____

   Example: Divide 2000 ÷ 2 ÷ 2 ÷ 2 ÷ 2

   Enter: [2] [0] [0] [0] [÷] [2] [Enter/=] | 1000 |

   =

          | 500 |

   =

          | 250 |

   =

   [Enter/=] | 125 |

7. Divide 1536 ÷ 4 ÷ 4 ÷ 4 ÷ 4

   _____ _____ _____ _____

8. Camille had 96 cookies and wanted to share them with her 12 friends. If she gave herself and her friends the same number of cookies, how many cookies did Camille and each of her friends get?

   _____

20   © Harcourt Achieve Inc. and Stephen Hake. All rights reserved.   Saxon Math

Fractions and Decimals 6

• Convert Fractions to Decimal Values

Teacher's Guide

Vocabulary:

Numerator, denominator, mixed number, improper fraction, decimal value, "parts of the whole," "(number) out of (total)"

"The number we are counting (numerator) divided by the number of equal parts of the whole (denominator)"

Example: $\frac{3}{8}$: "We are counting 3 divided by 8 equal parts" or "We count the numerator, 3, divided by the denominator, 8"

Operation:

On a basic 4-function calculator, fractions become simple division problems. Fractions become decimals by entering the numerator number, the division key ($\div$), and the denominator number. We can explore the many identities of a fraction: the parts of a whole, a division problem, or a decimal number.

Tips:

Remind students that when fractions are converted to decimal form, they may still be considered fractions of a whole.

For example, $\frac{1}{8}$ is converted to decimal form of 0.125. This is the same as $\frac{125}{1000}$. This may be useful to further instruct students on place value, division, simplifying fractions and other mathematical purposes.

When working with mixed numbers (e.g. $2\frac{3}{4}$), instruct students to convert the mixed number to an improper fraction (e.g. $\frac{11}{4}$), or enter the fractional part of the number first then the = key, then the + key followed by the whole number.

Saxon Math   © Harcourt Achieve Inc. and Stephen Hake. All rights reserved.   21

Fractions and Decimals 6

Guided Practice

Fractions become simple division problems in the calculator.

Fractions and mixed numbers (a whole number plus a fraction) can be represented as decimal numbers. For example, $\frac{3}{4}$ is the same as 0.75.

Money can give us good examples of how fractions and decimals mean the same thing: **parts of a whole**.

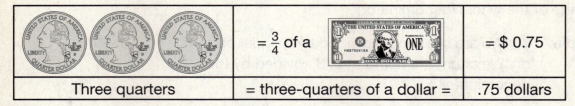

To convert a fraction, enter its numerator (top number), then the divide symbol (÷), then the denominator (bottom number) of the fraction, and then the = key.

Example 1: Convert $\frac{1}{2}$ to decimal value

    1 ÷ 2 [Enter/=]   0.5

The decimal value of $\frac{1}{2}$ is **0.5**

When working with mixed numbers (**ex. $2\frac{3}{4}$**), convert the mixed number to an irregular fraction (**ex. $\frac{11}{4}$**) or enter the fractional part of the number first, then the = key, then the plus key and the whole number to add the two sets of numbers.

Example: Find the decimal value of $1\frac{3}{8}$

Solution 1: Use the improper form of $1\frac{3}{8}$ or $\frac{11}{8}$.

Enter:

   1.375

Solution 2: Enter the fraction, then add the whole number:

Enter:

3 ÷ 8 + 1 Enter= | 1.375

Example 2: Convert $1\frac{3}{5}$ to decimal value.

Since the 1 will be the same in decimal value, we work only with the fraction:

3 ÷ 5 Enter= | 0.6

Add the 1 to the fraction:

+ 1 Enter= | 1.6

The decimal value of $1\frac{3}{5}$ is **1.6**.

Name _____

Fractions and Decimals 6

Practice Worksheet

Change the following fractions into their equivalent decimals.

Examples: Change $\frac{4}{5}$ into a decimal.

Enter: $4 \div 5 =$

[4] [÷] [5] [Enter =] ⟶ | 0.8 |

Change $3\frac{1}{4}$ into a decimal.

Enter: $1 \div 4 + 3 =$

[1] [÷] [4] [+] [3] [Enter =] ⟶ | 3.25 |

or enter: $13 \div 4 =$

[1] [3] [÷] [4] [Enter =] ⟶ | 3.25 |

1. $\frac{1}{2} =$ _____

2. $\frac{3}{10} =$ _____

3. $\frac{3}{8} =$ _____

4. $\frac{1}{6} =$ _____

5. $\frac{2}{3} =$ _____

6. $1\frac{1}{4} =$ _____

7. $3\frac{3}{5} =$ _____

8. $2\frac{5}{8} =$ _____

9. $3\frac{4}{9} =$ _____

10. How much money would you have if you had $\frac{3}{5}$ of a dollar?

_____

11. Jorge needs \$1.30 to buy a notebook for school. His mother said she would lend him $\frac{2}{5}$ of a dollar and $\frac{7}{10}$ of a dollar. How much money will his mother lend him? How much more money will he need to buy the notebook?

_____

Multiplying and Dividing Fractions · 7

Teacher's Guide

Vocabulary:

numerator, denominator, factor, product, dividend, divisor, quotient, reciprocal (inverse)

Operation:

Fractions are not supported on a basic calculator and are converted to decimal form by entering the numerator number, the division key ($\div$), and the denominator number.

Students should be able to convert mixed numbers into improper fractions mentally.

Emphasize the importance of converting division problems into multiplication by the reciprocal (inverse) of the fraction that comes after the $\div$.

Example: Divide $\frac{1}{4} \div \frac{2}{3}$

Have students restate the problem as $\frac{1}{4} \times \frac{3}{2}$

$\boxed{1}$ $\boxed{\div}$ $\boxed{4}$ $\boxed{\text{x}}$ $\boxed{3}$ $\boxed{\div}$ $\boxed{2}$ $\boxed{\text{Enter}\atop=}$

$$\boxed{0.375}$$

The answer 0.375 is the decimal equivalent to $\frac{3}{8}$.

The supplementary material will include exercises involving multiplication and division of fractions that utilize the memory functions after students gain mastery of the memory functions.

Saxon Math   © Harcourt Achieve Inc. and Stephen Hake. All rights reserved.   25

Multiplying and Dividing Fractions 7

Guided Practice

Multiplying a fraction times a whole number:

The basic 4-function calculator will not display fractions in a numerator over denominator format. To make calculations using fractions such as $\frac{1}{3}$ times 21, we must remember to enter and calculate the decimal value of the fraction before multiplying the whole number.

Example 1: Multiply $\frac{1}{4} \times 96$

We will enter the fraction $\frac{1}{4}$ first and convert it to its decimal equivalent. Then we can multiply the decimal times 96.

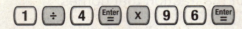

| 24 |

96 multiplied by $\frac{1}{4}$ is 24

Multiplying a fraction times a fraction:

To make calculations using fractions such as $\frac{1}{3}$ times $\frac{1}{4}$, we must remember to enter and calculate the decimal value of the first fraction first before multiplying the second fraction.

Example 2: Multiply $\frac{1}{4} \times \frac{1}{3}$

We will enter the fraction $\frac{1}{4}$ first and convert it to its decimal equivalent. Then we can multiply the decimal value times 1 divided by 3.

[1] [÷] [4] [Enter/=] [x] [1] [÷] [3] [Enter/=]

| 0.0833333 |

$\frac{1}{4} \times \frac{1}{3}$ is 0.083333... the decimal equivalent of $\frac{1}{12}$

Dividing Fractions:

Overview:

Basic calculators are not designed for direct entry of a fraction calculation. For example, $3 \div \frac{1}{3}$ will give you the incorrect answer of 1.0 The calculator sees two steps to this input that we must correct.

26 © Harcourt Achieve Inc. and Stephen Hake. All rights reserved. **Saxon Math**

Multiplying and Dividing Fractions 7

Example: Divide: $6 \div \frac{2}{3}$

Solution: This solution uses the inverse relationship of multiplication and division. We may think of the inverse of a fraction as its "flip" side. The fraction $\frac{2}{3}$ "flipped" becomes $\frac{3}{2}$. $\frac{1}{4}$ becomes $\frac{4}{1}$.

To divide 6 by $\frac{2}{3}$, we can **enter the inverse of $\frac{2}{3}$ and multiply.**

Step 1: "Flip" $\frac{2}{3}$ in our minds to become $\frac{3}{2}$.

Step 2: Multiply $6 \times \frac{3}{2}$

(6) (x) (3) (÷) (2) (Enter =) | 9 |

Mixed Numbers

Example 2: Divide: $8 \div 2\frac{2}{3}$

To use the inverse of a mixed number such as $2\frac{2}{3}$ we must first convert the mixed number to an improper fraction. $2\frac{2}{3} = \frac{8}{3}$

We can now multiply 8 by the inverse of $\frac{8}{3}$ or $\frac{3}{8}$

(8) (x) (3) (÷) (8) (Enter =) | 3 |

Saxon Math   © Harcourt Achieve Inc. and Stephen Hake. All rights reserved.   27

Name _____

Multiplying and Dividing Fractions   7

Practice Worksheet

Multiply using your calculator.

Example: Multiply $\frac{1}{4} \times 32$

Enter: 1 ÷ 4 = × 32 =

[1] [÷] [4] [Enter =] [x] [3] [2] [Enter =] | 8 |

Example: Multiply $\frac{2}{3} \times \frac{3}{4}$

Enter: 2 ÷ 3 = × 3 ÷ 4 =

[2] [÷] [3] [Enter =] [x] [3] [÷] [4] [Enter =] | 0.5 |

1. $\frac{1}{3} \times 12 =$ _____

2. $\frac{1}{5} \times 25 =$ _____

3. $\frac{1}{2} \times 36 =$ _____

4. $\frac{5}{8} \times \frac{4}{5} =$ _____

5. $\frac{1}{2} \times \frac{2}{5} =$ _____

6. $\frac{5}{24} \times \frac{8}{25} =$ _____

Divide using your calculator.

Example: Divide $\frac{2}{3} \div \frac{5}{6}$

Enter: 2 ÷ 3 × 6 ÷ 5 =

[2] [÷] [3] [x] [6] [÷] [5] [Enter =] | 0.799999 |

Example: Divide $1\frac{1}{4} \div 1\frac{1}{2}$

Change to improper fractions: $\frac{5}{4} \div \frac{3}{2}$

Enter: 5 ÷ 4 × 2 ÷ 3 =

[5] [÷] [4] [x] [2] [÷] [3] [Enter =] | 0.833333 |

7. $\frac{3}{4} \div \frac{2}{3} =$ _____

8. $\frac{1}{2} \div \frac{1}{4} =$ _____

9. $\frac{5}{8} \div \frac{1}{3} =$ _____

10. $1\frac{1}{4} \div 2\frac{1}{2} =$ _____

11. $1\frac{3}{4} \div 3\frac{1}{2} =$ _____

12. $3\frac{3}{8} \div 1\frac{1}{8} =$ _____

28   © Harcourt Achieve Inc. and Stephen Hake. All rights reserved.   *Saxon Math*

Order of Operations and Memory — 8

Teacher's Guide

Vocabulary:

Memory, recall

Operation:

The basic 4-function calculator will perform operations in the order in which they are typed, rather than in strict order of operations.

Example: Add: $3 + \frac{3}{6}$

If we enter:

【3】【+】【3】【÷】【6】【Enter =】 | 1 |

Our answer is incorrect.

We must complete the fraction's conversion to decimal before adding it to the whole number.

Enter: $3 \div 6 + 3 =$

【3】【÷】【6】【+】【3】【Enter =】 | 3.5 |

The **Memory Plus (M+)**, **Minus (M-)**, and **Recall (MRc)** buttons are useful tools for your students when working with problems that call for more than one step, particularly operations with mixed fractions. Any number in the display is added to memory by using the **Memory Plus** button or subtracted from Memory using the **Memory Minus** button. The Memory Recall button completes the problem by adding the two numbers in memory together.

Example: Add: $2\frac{1}{2} + 3\frac{3}{4} =$

Enter:

【1】【÷】【2】【+】【2】【M+】 | 2.5 |

【3】【÷】【4】【+】【3】【M+】 | 3.75 |

【MRc】 | 6.25 |

Saxon Math   © Harcourt Achieve Inc. and Stephen Hake. All rights reserved.   29

Guided Practice

When you use a calculator to solve math problems that take more than one step, it is important to do things completely and in the right order.

Example 1: When Chondra went to the market, she bought 3 apples from one fruit stand, 4 apples from a second fruit stand, 2 apples from a third fruit stand, and 3 apples from a fourth fruit stand.

When she went home, she divided the apples between herself and her two sisters. How many apples did each girl get?

To solve this problem we add all the apples and the divide by 3, the number of persons including Chondra and her sisters. We must be careful how we do this.

We enter: 3 + 4 + 2 + 3 ÷ 3 =

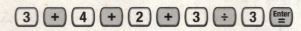

| 4 |

Each girl received **4 apples**.

Example 2: Add: $2 + \frac{3}{4}$

If we enter:

| 1.25 |

Our answer is incorrect.

We must complete the fraction's conversion to decimal before adding it to the whole number.

Enter: 3 ÷ 4 + 2 =

| 2.75 |

The correct answer is 2.75 or $2\frac{3}{4}$.

Memory Function

There are three memory function buttons on a basic calculator:

Order of Operations and Memory **8**

M+	The **Memory Plus** button is used to add a number to memory. Any number that is displayed may be added to memory using this button. If there is already a number in memory, using the Memory Plus button again **will add** the number on your display to the number already in memory.
M-	The **Memory Minus** button is used to subtract a number from a number already in memory. Whatever number is on the current display will be subtracted from the memory value when you use this key. The Memory Minus button may also be used to clear memory by entering the exact amount of the number already in memory and using Memory Minus.
MRc	The **Memory Retrieve** button is used to call up the number in memory to start a calculation or in the middle of a calculation.

Example: Tony baked 24 cookies, 12 brownies and 16 cupcakes for the bake sale. By noon he had sold $\frac{1}{2}$ of his cookies, $\frac{1}{4}$ of his brownies and $\frac{3}{8}$ of his cupcakes. How many items in total did he sell?

Step 1: $\frac{1}{2}$ of 24

[1] [÷] [2] [x] [2] [4] [Enter =] | 12 |

Add to Memory [M+]

Step 2: $\frac{1}{4}$ of 12

[1] [÷] [4] [x] [1] [2] [Enter =] | 3 |

Add to Memory [M+]

Step 3: $\frac{3}{8}$ of 16

[3] [÷] [8] [x] [1] [6] [Enter =] | 6 |

Add to Memory [M+]

Step 4: Retrieve Solution:

[MRc] | 21 |

The solution, 21, is displayed.

Saxon Math   © Harcourt Achieve Inc. and Stephen Hake. All rights reserved.   **31**

Name _____ **Order of Operations and Memory** (8)

Practice Worksheet

Perform the following calculations on your calculator.

Example: Add $5 + \frac{1}{4}$

Enter: $1 \div 4 + 5 =$

[1] [÷] [4] [+] [5] [Enter/=] | 5.25 |

1. $2 + \frac{1}{2} =$ _____   **2.** $4 + \frac{2}{3} =$ _____   **3.** $3 + \frac{3}{4} =$ _____

4. $8 + \frac{3}{5} =$ _____   **5.** $9 + 5/6 =$ _____   **6.** $12 + \frac{7}{8} =$ _____

Add the following mixed fractions. Use your memory function.

Example: Add $2\frac{3}{5} + 3\frac{1}{4}$

Enter: $3 \div 5 + 2$, then Add to Memory

[3] [÷] [5] [+] [2] [M+] | 2.6 |

$1 \div 4 + 3$, then Add to Memory

[1] [÷] [4] [+] [3] [M+] | 3.25 |

[MRC] | 5.85 |

7. $2\frac{1}{4} + 3\frac{1}{2} =$ _____   **8.** $5\frac{3}{8} + 3\frac{1}{8} =$ _____

9. $4\frac{3}{5} + 5\frac{2}{5} =$ _____   **10.** $8\frac{3}{4} + 3\frac{2}{3} =$ _____

11. $9\frac{1}{3} + 10\frac{1}{3} =$ _____   **12.** $12\frac{5}{8} + 9\frac{1}{4} =$ _____

Area and Volume 9

Teacher's Guide

Vocabulary:
Rows, columns, height, length, width, square units, cubic units

Operation:
For simple area calculations, the student will multiply length × width, or number of rows × number of columns. Volume is the calculation of length × width × height.

Tips:
For more complex calculations, use of the memory function can be useful.

Example: What is the area of the colored units? What fraction of the square does the colored portion represent in decimal form?

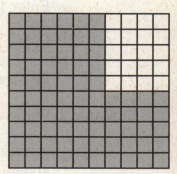

Solution: We can find area by multiplying the lower 10 columns by 5 and placing that value in memory, then multiplying 6 columns time 5 adding that to existing memory, then retrieving the sum.

	50
	30
	80

The area is 80 units.

To find the fraction of the whole, we first must determine the whole's area.

	100

There are 100 units in the square. Now we divide by the number of colored units by the whole area.

	.8

The answer is .8 or $\frac{8}{10}$.

Saxon Math © Harcourt Achieve Inc. and Stephen Hake. All rights reserved. 33

Guided Practice

Example 1: Area

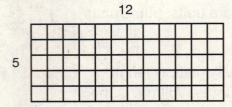

What is the area of the rectangle shown above?

To find the area, we multiply the number of columns times the number of rows: 12 × 5.

Enter 12 × 5 =

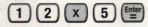

| 60 |

The area of the rectangle is **60 square units**.

Example 2: Volume

What is the volume of the rectangular prism shown below?

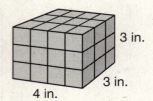

To find the volume we will count to see how many rows and columns there are in one layer and how many layers are in the rectangle. When we count we see the object is 4 blocks long, 3 blocks wide and there are 3 layers. We will multiply 4 times 3 times 3.

| 36 |

The prism has a volume of **80 cubic units**.

Example 3: Arrays

Area and Volume 9

Here are three arrays of objects. The total number of objects is equal to the product of which two numbers?

    A 7 × 8   **B** 7 × 7   **C** 6 × 7   **D** 6 × 6

We can use the calculator to find the number of objects in the arrays and we can also use it to check each of the products to find a match.

There are 5 columns and 5 rows of squares in the first array. We can call this a 5 × 5 array. We multiply the number of columns by the number of rows to find the total number of squares:

[5] [×] [5] [Enter =]   25

The next array is a 3 × 2 array of stars. The total number of stars is:

[3] [×] [2] [Enter =]   6

The next array is a 6 × 3 array of circles. The total number of circles is:

[6] [×] [3] [Enter =]   18

To find the total number of objects in the arrays we add:

25 + 6 + 18 =

[2][5] [+] [6] [+] [1][8] [Enter =]   49

To find the multiplication that equals our answer of 49 we check each choice until we get to the correct one

    A 7 × 8 = [7] [×] [8] [Enter =]   56

    B 7 × 7 = [7] [×] [7] [Enter =]   49

    C 6 × 7 = [6] [×] [7] [Enter =]   42

    D 6 × 6 = [6] [×] [6] [Enter =]   36

Choice **B** gives us the correct result of 49. We choose **B** for our answer.

Saxon Math

Name _____

Area and Volume 9
Practice Worksheet

Calculate the areas of the rectangles below.

1. 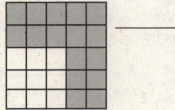 _____

2. 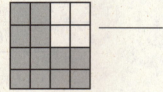 _____

What is the area of the shaded region? What fraction of the square does the shaded region represent in decimal form?

3. 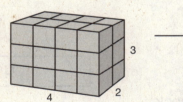 _____

4. 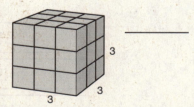 _____

Calculate the volumes of the rectangular prisms below.

5. _____

6. _____

7. Randall needs to buy a tablecloth for his kitchen table. He measures the length and width of the tabletop and finds that it measures 3 feet by 8 feet. What is the area of Randall's tabletop?

_____

36
© Harcourt Achieve Inc. and Stephen Hake. All rights reserved.
Saxon Math

Supplementary Exercises 10

Teacher's Guide

The following exercises provide practice in the concepts described throughout this manual. Use the lesson correspondence to determine which exercises are appropriate at different stages of students' progress. Since no guidance is given for how to complete any of the exercises, students will be expected to know how to use their calculators to aid their problem solving.

Individual problems may be chosen and completed by the entire class if there is extra time at the end of a lesson, or could be given to accelerated learners who finish assigned work early. The supplementary material could also serve as an "end of year" test of students' mathematical and calculator skills.

Saxon Math © Harcourt Achieve Inc. and Stephen Hake. All rights reserved. 37

Name _____   **Supplementary Exercises** **10**
Practice Worksheet

1. In which number sentence does 7 make the sentence true?

   A 21 ÷ ☐ = 7   B 21 ÷ 3 = ☐

   C ☐ × 21 = 7   D ☐ ÷ 7 = 21

2. Arrange these fractions in order from greatest to least.

   _____

   A $\frac{1}{2}$ B $\frac{2}{5}$ C $\frac{3}{8}$ D $\frac{4}{6}$

3. The school hockey team has won 16 of its 24 games. What fraction of its games did the team win?

   A $\frac{5}{8}$ B $\frac{3}{4}$ C $\frac{2}{3}$ D $\frac{8}{16}$

4. Moira decorated $\frac{5}{8}$ of her design. Which decimal represents the decorated portion of her design?

   A 0.5800   B 0.600

   C 0.625   D 0.8585

5. Harry has to build a model. The plans call for a piece that is $\frac{3}{10}$ of an inch. Harry only has a standard ruler. What fraction of an inch is closest to the measure he needs?

   A $\frac{3}{8}$ B $\frac{1}{2}$ C $\frac{3}{4}$ D $\frac{1}{4}$

6. Rhonda and Darlene were making walnut cookies. Rhonda's recipe called for $\frac{2}{3}$ cup of walnuts. Darlene's recipe called for $\frac{9}{16}$ cup of walnuts. Which shows the correct relationship of these fractions?

   A $\frac{9}{16} > \frac{2}{3}$ B $\frac{2}{3} < \frac{9}{16}$ C $\frac{2}{3} = \frac{9}{16}$ D $\frac{2}{3} > \frac{9}{16}$

7. It takes Britney 10 minutes to walk to school each day. At this rate, how many days will it take Britney to spend 60 minutes walking to school?

   A 4 days   B 5 days   C 6 days   D 9 days

© Harcourt Achieve Inc. and Stephen Hake. All rights reserved.

Saxon Math

Name _____

Supplementary Exercises 10
Practice Worksheet (cont.)

8. The school auditorium has 99 seats. People are sitting in 68 of the seats. Which is the best estimate of the number of seats that do NOT have people sitting in them?

   A 170   **B** 30   **C** 20   **D** 100

9. The table below shows the number of rectangular prisms and the number of faces on these rectangular prisms.

   If you have 16 rectangular prisms, how many faces will there be?

   A 114

   B 92

   C 64

   D 96

Number of Rectangular Prisms	Number of Faces
4	24
8	48
12	72

10. A box contains 9 oranges. Boxes have been stacked in piles in a warehouse. Which list below shows the number of oranges that could be in a stack of boxes?

    A 27, 62, 18, 9, or 63

    B 9, 28, 45, 54, or 27

    C 63, 36, 18, 54, or 27

    D 73, 9, 25, 36, or 18

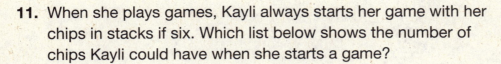

11. When she plays games, Kayli always starts her game with her chips in stacks if six. Which list below shows the number of chips Kayli could have when she starts a game?

    A 60, 54, 16, or 12

    B 12, 18, 72, or 54

    C 24, 28, 16, or 2

    D 38, 24, 6, or 16

Saxon Math

Name _____

Supplementary Exercises 10

Practice Worksheet (cont.)

12. Carl drew three parallelograms. He then measured their perimeters.

Parallelogram	1	2	3	4	5	6
Perimeter	6	11	16			

If the pattern of perimeters continues as he draws three more parallelograms, what will the perimeter of the sixth parallelogram be?

A 22   **B** 31   **C** 36   **D** 26

13. Koji is working on the graph shown below. He knows there were 30 babies born in March at Smithville Hospital.

January	
February	
March	

Key = 5 babies.

How many more babies does Koji need to add to March to finish the graph?

A 3   **B** 5   **C** 27   **D** 6

40   © Harcourt Achieve Inc. and Stephen Hake. All rights reserved.   *Saxon Math*

Answers

Addition (p. 2–4)

1. 119
2. 96
3. 154
4. 77
5. 103
6. 63
7. 28
8. 27, 32, 37
9. 21, 28, 35

   25 cans

Subtraction (p. 5–7)

1. 45
2. 58
3. 22
4. 11
5. 79
6. 21
7. 0
8. 69
9. 9
10. 12
11. 17, 12, 7
12. 28, 21, 14

Money (p. 8–12)

1. $1061.22
2. $109.82
3. $1.82
4. $405.36
5. D
6. C

Multiplication (p. 13–17)

1. 30
2. 12
3. 56
4. 625
5. 900
6. 473
7. 32, 128, 512, 2048
8. B
9. C

Yards	Feet	Inches		Feet	Inches
1	3	36		1	12
2	6	72		2	24
3	9	108		3	36
4	12	144		4	48
5	15	180		5	60

Gallons	Quarts	Pints		Pounds	Ounces
1	4	8		1	16
2	8	16		2	32
3	12	24		3	48
4	16	32		4	64
5	20	40		5	80

Division (p. 18–20)

1. 4
2. 3
3. 10
4. 9
5. 12
6. 35
7. 384, 96, 24, 6
8. 8 cookies

Fractions and Decimals (p. 21–24)

1. 0.5
2. 0.3

Saxon Math

Answers

3. 0.375

4. 0.1667

5. 0.6667

6. 1.25

7. 3.6

8. 2.625

9. 3.4444

10. $0.60 or 60 cents

11. She will lend him $0.90 or 90 cents.

    He still needs $0.40 or 40 cents.

Multiplying and Dividing Fractions (p. 25–28)

1. 4

2. 5

3. 18

4. 0.5

5. 0.2

6. 0.0667

7. 1.125

8. 2

9. 1.875

10. 0.5

11. 0.5

12. 3

Order of Operations and Memory (p. 29–32)

1. 2.5

2. 4.6667

3. 3.75

4. 8.6

5. 9.8333

6. 12.875

7. 5.75

8. 8.5

9. 10

10. 12.4167

11. 19.6667

12. 21.875

Area and Volume (p. 33–36)

1. 15 square units

2. 14 square units

3. 16 square units;

   0.64 of the whole

4. 12 square units;

   0.75 of the whole

5. 24 cubic units

6. 27 cubic units

7. 24 square feet

Supplementary Exercises (p. 37–40)

1. B

2. CBAD

3. C

4. C

5. D

6. D

7. C

8. B

9. D

10. C

11. B

12. B

13. A

42   © Harcourt Achieve Inc. and Stephen Hake. All rights reserved.   *Saxon Math*